BRAND *with* GRACE
Journal

DESIGN BY TECH WITH TASHA

BRAND *with* GRACE
Journal

by

Tasha Glover

CONTENTS

ABOUT THE AUTHOR

Tasha Glover is a Grace Empowered mentor, visionary, and Business Strategist dedicated to helping believers uncover their true kingdom identity and walk boldly in their God-given mandate. As the founder of Brand with Grace, she has spent years guiding individuals and businesses to align their calling with God's divine strategy, reminding them that their return on obedience is always greater than their return on investment.

Through her work, Tasha empowers others to discern God's voice, overcome identity blockers like competition and false humility, and confidently steward the influence they have been entrusted with. She believes that building with stones—God-ordained principles rather than fleeting trends—creates a lasting impact that expands His Kingdom.

Hi, I'm Tasha Glover

INTRODUCTION

BRAND *with* GRACE is...

a process and experience of unveiling the true authentic representation of your Kingdom identity.

It's how you show up every day. It's not a former or future version of what you want to be known for. It's building on the vision that God has given you about who you are and what you represent. It's operating in the gift(s) you're called to steward during your lifespan with God's leading and power.

And God said to me:

"People are branding what they
want to become and not what
I called them to be."

The world teaches you to brand
by becoming what or who
you want to be.

You brand how you want people to see you and
what you want to be known for. You're taught to
speak the language of your ideal client and to
know all about their needs.

Brand with Grace will challenge the way you
were taught to brand.

How is creating a brand with grace different?

Think of branding with the grace of God as being yielded to His Spirit. You're yielded to whatever He wants you to do with whatever it is He's calling you to create in the earth. Also, when I speak about a brand, I'm not just speaking personal brand. Your brand could be your business, service, or program.

It could be something new or another leg or tier of what God is calling you to create. It's the identity of what God has called you to steward in the earth

HEARING FROM GOD

Do you hear from God?

"BUT SEEK FIRST THE KINGDOM OF GOD AND HIS RIGHTEOUSNESS, AND ALL THESE THINGS SHALL BE ADDED TO YOU." MATTHEW 6:33

Your confidence in your ability to hear God is vital to every aspect of your life, because your ability to hear God enables you to make wise decisions. It helps you to operate from a place of wisdom where the Holy Spirit is present with you, guiding you, and giving you new, creative ideas.

Hearing from God

What challenges, if any, do you have discerning God's voice?

☐ YES   ☐ NO

Hearing from God

Share a time where God gave you specific instructions or answers.

Hearing from God

When was the last time you met with Jesus?

WEEKLY
Spiritual Exercises

- ☐ Decree aloud: "I have the ability to discern God's voice."

- ☐ Find time to sit with the Lord without expectations.

- ☐ Invite God into your space numerous times throughout the day.

- ☐ Repeat this question to God: "God, what is my mandate?"

- ☐ Journal with the Lord, ask Him open-ended questions, and write down what He says.

- ☐ Ask God where He is in your (________). Fill in the blank.

HEARING FROM GOD
Invitation

Read Acts 22 in three translations.

Focus on believing God for your own divine encounter with Him—one that will get you on the path to fulfilling your destiny.

Hearing God Invitation

What is your mandate?

notes

notes

notes

notes

DATE

notes

notes

notes

notes

RESPONDING TO GOD

Do you respond to God?

Although we all, as believers, should have a reverent fear of the Lord, sometimes we can find ourselves in a state of near paralysis when it comes to responding to God.

Responding to God is tied to our relationship with Him and us beginning to see the different aspects of Himself He reveals to us. He is, in fact, our Lord and our Savior. He is El Shaddai, the covering over our heads. But, He is also our friend and our Father.

Responding to God

What challenges, if any, do you have
responding to God's voice?

Are you in dialogue with God?

☐ YES   ☐ NO

Responding to God

Share a time when God gave you specific instructions or answers.

Responding to God

When was the last time you met Jesus?

WEEKLY
Spiritual Exercises

- ☐ Decree aloud: I have the ability to discern God's voice.

- ☐ Find time to sit with the Lord without expectations.

- ☐ Invite God into your space numerous times throughout the day.

- ☐ Repeat this question to God: "God what is my mandate?"

- ☐ Journal with the Lord, ask Him open-ended questions, and write down what He says.

- ☐ Ask God where He is in your (   ) fill in the blank.

RESPONDING TO GOD
Invitation

☐ Recall a time that God has spoken to you where you did not respond to what you heard.

☐ Take the time to sit with God and respond to Him around those things. Journal what God says to you and implement the strategies.

Responding to God

What challenges came up for you?

notes

notes

notes

notes

DATE

notes

DATE

notes

DATE

notes

DATE

notes

DATE

UNCOVER YOUR TRUE KINGDOM IDENTITY

When you know what your message is, you know who you're speaking to. When you know what the goal is and what the desired result is, you know what success looks like. You can work in and define excellence in what you're called to do. When you're powered by Holy Spirit, you work in God's grace and when it gets difficult, you won't give up.

How to start and build on a firm foundation

Living within you is the Christ who floods you with the expectation of glory! This mystery of Christ, embedded within us, becomes a heavenly treasure chest of hope filled with the riches of glory for His people. And God wants everyone to know it. Christ is our message! We preach to awaken hearts and bring every person into the full understanding of truth. It has become my inspiration and passion in ministry to labor with a tireless intensity, with His power flowing through me to present to every believer the revelation of being His perfect one in Jesus Christ.

YOUR FOUNDATION STARTS
with kingdom identity

Paul was confident in his identity and knew the results and purpose of what he was called to do. Let's use this scripture and break it down into parts, so you can write your own kingdom identity. Keep in mind, if you have several services and programs, this may be different for each one. Repeat this process for each new idea that is birthed along your journey.

PAUL'S KINGDOM IDENTITY:

MESSAGE:

Living within you is the Christ who floods you with the expectation of glory! This mystery of Christ, embedded within us, becomes a heavenly treasure chest of hope filled with the riches of glory for his people, and God wants everyone to know it. Christ is our message.

GOAL OF YOUR MESSAGE:

To awaken hearts

MEASUREMENT OF THE GOAL:

Every person having a full understanding
of the truth

INSPIRATION:

To present to every believer the revelation of being his perfect one in Jesus Christ.

PAUL'S KINGDOM IDENTITY:

PASSION:

To present to every believer the revelation of being his perfect one in Jesus Christ (same as inspiration)

POWER:

To awaken hearts

As you see from the kingdom identity of Paul listed above, he was clear about how God wanted to use him. From this identity, we also understand the importance of inspiration and passion. Paul was propelled by the result of what he was delivering and powered by God's spirit to do as much as he could while he was on this earth.

USE THIS MODEL (COLOSSIANS 1:27-29)

TO WRITE YOUR KINGDOM IDENTITY:

USE THIS MODEL (COLOSSIANS 1:27-29)
TO WRITE YOUR KINGDOM IDENTITY:

USE THIS MODEL (COLOSSIANS 1:27-29)

TO WRITE YOUR KINGDOM IDENTITY:

BRAND *with* GRACE IS...

I think of it as a true authentic representation of your identity. It's how you show up every day. It's not a former or future version of what you want to be known for. It's building on the vision that God has shown you about who you are and what you represent. It's operating in the gift(s) you're called to steward during your lifespan with God's leading and power.

What does a true authentic representation of your brand look like? (This will evolve as you complete this journal, so come back to this at the end.)

What does a true authentic representation of your brand look like? (This will evolve as you complete this journal, so come back to this at the end.)

KEEP IN MIND...

The Kingdom of God is progressive. As part of the Kingdom, growth is expected. Keep in mind, there may be different versions of your brand over time, yet the foundation of your brand will not change.

Who did God call me to serve and not serve?

Uncover Your True Kingdom Identity

What problem did God call me to solve?

Uncover Your True Kingdom Identity

What transformation(s) does my brand bring?

Uncover Your True Kingdom Identity

What inspires me?

Uncover Your True Kingdom Identity

What am I passionate about?

Uncover Your True Kingdom Identity

What is my brand's mission?

Uncover Your True Kingdom Identity

How does God identify my brand?

Uncover Your True Kingdom Identity

What am I presenting?

Take your time writing out your kingdom identity.

Don't feel like you have to rush through any parts of this journal. Take your time writing out your brand identity and messaging. There are additional note sections included throughout this journal for you to record your responses as you sit with Holy Spirit.

Knowing what God says about what He's called you to do is essential because He's not going to change His mind. When you are sure of what God said, you can stand firm, no matter what the situation looks like

Again, It may take you some time just sitting with God and listening to be able to answer these questions. Take your time and don't rush through it. If you are not sure, just ask Him and be confident that the response you hear is the right one.

God wants you to know His thoughts and plans for you and your work. It's not a secret.

Believe what you hear

ISAIAH 43:10-11 (TPT)

You are my witnesses, my chosen servants. I chose you in order that you would know me intimately, believe me always, and fully understand that I am the only God. There was no god before me, and there will be no other god after me.

I, only I, am Yahweh, and there is no Savior-God but me.

UNCOVER YOUR TRUE KINGDOM IDENTITY

Invitation

- [ ] Sit with Holy Spirit around the truth about being created and being formed. Begin to write down the things that God gives you.

- [ ] Meditate on Psalm 139.

notes

notes

notes

DATE

notes

notes

notes

notes

notes

ROO ' ROI

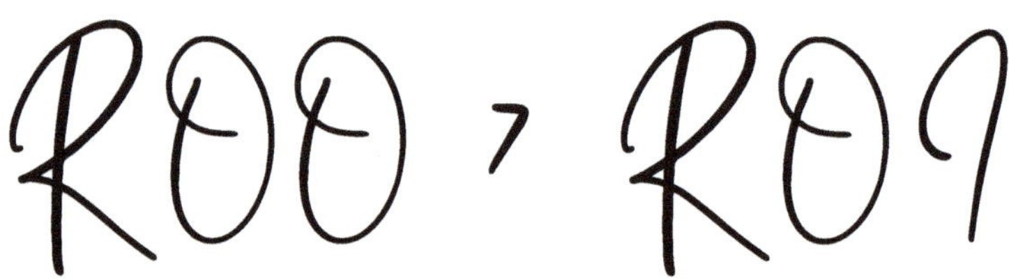

PSALM 119:12-14 (TPT)

My wonderful God, you are to be praised above all; teach me the power of your decrees.

I speak continually of your laws as I recite out loud your counsel to me.

I find more joy in following what you tell me to do than in chasing after all the wealth in the world.

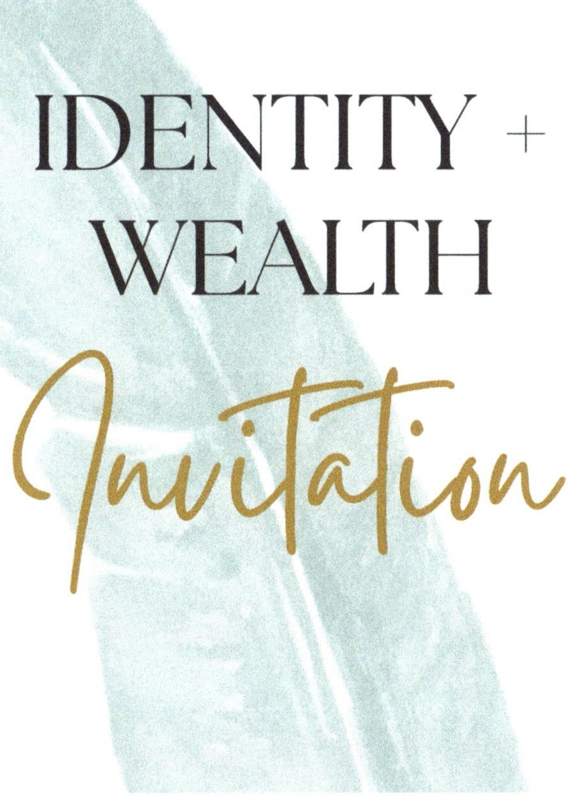

IDENTITY + WEALTH *Invitation*

☐ Read all of Psalm 119 in 3 translations.

☐ Meditate on your identity and the connection to wealth. What level of provision are you believing God for based on what He's assigned you to do in this season?

☐ Read all of Proverbs 8 in three translations.

DATE

notes

notes

DATE

notes

DATE

notes

DATE

DATE

notes

Your assignment is specific

2 CHRONICLES 31:20-21 (NLT)

In this way, King Hezekiah handled the distribution throughout all Judah, doing what was pleasing and good in the sight of the Lord his God.

In all that he did in the service of the Temple of God and in his efforts to follow God's law and commands, Hezekiah sought his God wholeheartedly. As a result, he was very successful.

IDENTITY + ALIGNMENT

Invitation

☐ Read II Chronicles 29 in three translations.

notes

notes

notes

notes

notes

notes

notes

notes

INFLUENCE

God will give you the
ability to influence and you
operate in that influence.

**INFLUENCE: The ability to affect others or events.
Also, the experience of being affected by someone
or something else.**

Every one of us has a sphere of influence and area in which
God has called us to serve. It is important to understand our
area(s) of influence and serve confidently and obediently.

PAUL'S AREA OF INFLUENCE:

ACTS 9:15 AMPC

But the Lord said to him, "Go, for this man is a chosen instrument of Mine to bear My name before the Gentiles and kings and the descendants of Israel."

ACTS 22:21 AMPC

And the Lord said to me, "Go, for I will send you far away unto the Gentiles (nations)."

Romans 15:20 AMPC

"Thus my ambition has been to preach the Gospel, not where Christ's name has already been known, lest I build on another man's foundation."

WHEN I WAS STARTING TO BUILD OUT TECH WITH TASHA, I WENT BACK TO GOD SEVERAL TIMES. "GOD, ARE YOU SURE?"

Because you said *digital marketing*. So… that sounds like this, but **is** that this? Am I supposed to target certain people?

Let me share that it was NOT what I could have imagined. Still, as my brand grows, there are layers being revealed. When it comes to knowing where and to whom we are sent, we have to get clarity from the One who whispers His secrets to us. We all have an area of influence and we will thrive when we serve from that place.

Influence

What influence did God give me?

Influence

What area did God call me to use my influence in?

Influence

What transformation does my influence bring?

LET'S TAKE ANOTHER LOOK AT AREAS OF INFLUENCE

When discussing influence, we're talking about calling—the specific areas where God has positioned us. Influence can manifest in three primary ways:

1. **Geographic:** A specific place God has called you to.
2. **Demographic:** The people or groups He's placed in your sphere.
3. **Sociographic:** Special interest groups or causes He's assigned to you.

For some people, it may be that you're called to your city and you're doing something on a local level. It may be a brick-and-mortar business. For other people, it may be more global, especially if you're online.

Your influence could lead you to several different areas or territories or close partnerships. Focus on understanding your sphere of influence and operate in what God says. Don't put limits on yourself based on what you think your reach is.

INFLUENCE
Invitation

	Ask a close friend or loved one where they think you are most effective. What areas of your life are they seeing the favor and anointing of God?

notes
DATE

notes

notes

notes

DATE

notes

notes

notes

notes

MESSAGING

Discover your messaging and serve it boldly.

Operate in your influence and don't focus so much on a niche.

Discover your message before you build out your visuals. Your message will reach who it needs to reach. Be confident in the areas that God has given you the wisdom, power, and authority to speak about.

ONE MANDATE, MANY MESSAGES, MANY METHODS

Mandate — Why you were sent.

The voice of your mandate. — *Message*

Method — How you serve your message.

MESSAGING

What topics do I speak about consistently?
Name at least three.

Now that you have a list of topics about which you are passionate, be intentional with how you show up to represent your messaging. You should be able to see a pattern in content. People will begin to identify you by what you consistently voice. Be okay with repetition—repetition is how we learn. Your messaging is something you're always speaking about and most likely repeat often.

MESSAGING

God is going to constantly fill your tank with information. You're not going to get bored with these topics. You will speak with revelation as you seek God for what He wants you to release.

Don't limit your voice to what's going on in the world. Kingdom entrepreneurs have the ability to tap into what God is doing in their industry. When you brand with grace, you continue to operate in whatever it is God is calling you to give out. Your messaging produces the content and your method for serving it to the world will develop.

Decree This...

I am Authentic, Authorized and Anointed!

Messaging

What has God called me to share about often?

Messaging

What am I led to teach, to impart, to nurture?

Messaging

What am I reading?

Messaging

What am I studying?

Messaging

What is God ministering to me the most
about in my life?

Messaging

What is my mandate?

Messaging

Of all my messages, what is the priority
to God in this season?

Messaging

What ways or methods am I using
to get my message(s) out?

Messaging

What new methods do I feel drawn to (i.e., social media, podcasting, writing)?

MESSAGING

Invitation

- [ ] Read 1 Chronicles 17 in three translations.

- [ ] Read John 5 in three translations.

- [ ] Consider the message you carry in life and in the marketplace. Meditate on the results of releasing that message.

DATE

notes

notes

notes

DATE

notes

notes

notes

VISUAL FOUNDATION

Develop your brand visually.

When you are developing your visuals, it's important to be creative.

Sit with your messaging and begin to flow in that creative process. If you could only describe without words and just visuals, where would you start? Here are some key visual parts of a brand.

VISUAL FOUNDATION

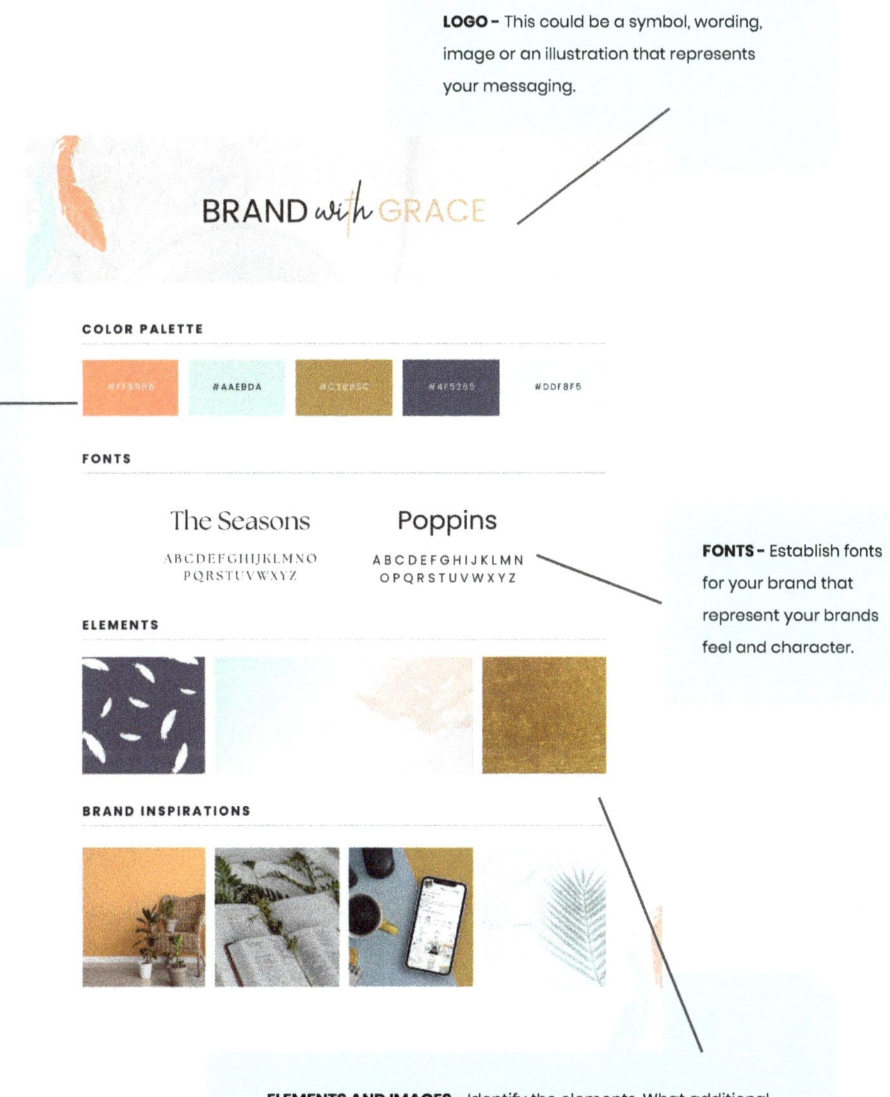

LOGO

COLORS

FONTS

ELEMENTS

BUILDING WITH STONES

Putting It All Together

It's time to continually build on the foundation of identity and intimacy.

We want to build with stones, and not with man-made bricks. Every insight and revelation that God is handing you are stones. What you are building must be tried in a fire and not fail. Evaluate what you are adding to your solid foundation and from where the information is coming. God does not build with man-made bricks, only living stones!

Build Carefully...

1 CORINTHIANS 3:10 (NLT)

Because of God's grace to me, I have laid
the foundation like an expert builder.
Now others are building on it. But whoever is
building on this foundation must be
very careful.

BUILDING WITH STONES

What season of building am I in (i.e., construction, preservation, restoration, rehabilitation, or reconstruction)?

BUILDING WITH STONES

If construction...
What is God calling me to build in this season?

BUILDING WITH STONES

If preservation...
What areas are working well and how am I maintaining them?

BUILDING WITH STONES

If restoration...
What area(s) need to be revived?

BUILDING WITH STONES

If reconstruction...
What areas need to be recreated and reframed?

BUILDING WITH STONES

If rehabilitation...

Do I have any man-made bricks in my foundation? What changes
can I make to replace them with living stones?

BUILDING WITH STONES

What is the specific strategy or instructions for my
current assignment?

BUILDING WITH STONES

What do I need to implement?

BUILDING WITH STONES

Who is God calling me to collaborate
with in this season?

BUILDING WITH STONES
Invitation

☐ Read and meditate on Exodus 25:31.

☐ Consider and ponder on how meticulous, specific and strategic God was with the building of the temple. Believe that God has specific instructions and strategies for what He has called you to build.

notes

notes

notes

notes

notes

notes

notes

notes

I hope you will take the time to sit with Holy Spirit and let Him speak to your heart as you journal together. Revelation will be unlocked and you will experience an increase in divine encounters and visitations from God. These encounters will lead you into greater intimacy with God and unlock the next steps of your journey to destiny.

Want a deeper dive into Brand with Grace?

Join us for in our Identity Immersion Mentorship Community.

You were created with a divine mandate—crafted by God with a unique kingdom identity, calling, and influence. But stepping into that identity with confidence requires clarity, alignment, and the wisdom to navigate the journey.

In *Brand with Grace: Uncover Your True Kingdom Identity*, Tasha Glover walks you through **The Identity Pathway**, a Spirit-led process designed to help you hear God clearly, respond in obedience, and align every area of your life and work with His Kingdom agenda.

GET YOUR COPY!